The Best of Li'l ABNER

The Best of Li'l ABNER

AL CAPP

Holt, Rinehart and Winston / New York

For my sister, Madelaine Capp Gardner

Published simultaneously in Canada by Holt, Rinehart
and Winston of Canada, Limited.

Library of Congress Catalog Card Number: 78-53782
ISBN Hardbound: 0-03-044071-8
ISBN Paperback: 0-03-045516-2

First Edition

Printed in the United States of America

10 9 8 7 6 5 4 3 2 1

Contents

Introduction

This book begins when I was a hungry, eager art student of twenty-four and ends when I am sixty-eight. In between, I wrote and illustrated stories that several million Americans read.

I would always begin my stories with "What if . . . ?" What if, for instance, a Dogpatcher digging in to plant a trash-bean tree came upon a shapely leg, then another one, and then the full, lush figure of a seventeen-year-old, who, as she was exposed to sunlight, woke up breathing and smiling? What if an archaeologist, rushed in from the nearby state university, declared it was a miracle. She is Leif Ericsson's kid sister, Tenderleif, the only survivor, buried in the ice when her boat sank—and the minute she sees Li'l Abner she begins breathing hard. "She is seventeen years old," explains Mammy, "and she haint had a date fo' four hundred years!"

Now, what if there were a special day in Dogpatch in which any bachelor, caught by any lady before sundown, must marry her (except for ladies over a hundred, who are entitled to any boy they want)? What if we all know that Daisy Mae is incurably smitten with Abner and will die if anyone else nabs him? We would always find some way to get him out of it, but one time there was no way to get him out of it. No human way. We sat around, paralyzed—until it came to me. "This is our world," I cried. "We can do anything we want. If human ways won't work—let's try SUPERHUMAN ways!" From then on our endings came a lot easier.

And that's the way it went. We piled one "What if" on another. We had a marvelous time. Let me explain why I say "we." I did not do my comic strips alone. Today, comic strips are reduced to the size of a row of postage stamps, and the cartoonist has to find some hobby for those extra three days. In 1934, however, you were required to fill six columns of daily space, and a full, color page on Sunday that was divided into three parts. And so, in 1934, I began by hiring the first two artists I interviewed, Andy Amato and Harvey Curtis. Andy turned out to be as brilliant a man as I know, Harvey one of the cleverest. They worked with me from the beginning of *Li'l Abner* to its end.

Why was he "Li'l Abner," six feet three and nineteen years old? Why was his family so poverty-stricken, his town a disaster area too poor to pay any taxes and too

proud to accept any government help? One of the rewards of doing a comic strip is that it gives you a chance to redraw your own childhood. Luckily, there was mighty little in mine that couldn't take redrawing. We were poorer than any family today. We had no welfare, no food stamps, none of the sort of things that, today, every wretched family has. In my childhood, I was told about "work relief." I ran home to tell my mother. She looked at me sternly. "That," she said, "is for poor people."

My mother and father had been brought to this country from Russia when they were infants. Their fathers found that the great promise of America was true—it was no crime to be a Jew. Naturally, the kids in the street mocked you, you knew better than to ask for employment for any jobs non-Jews might want, and, of course, you lived in the Jewish ghetto. This cost a few pennies more, but it was worth it to live with one's own people. Yet somewhere, written down, you had all the rights anyone else had, and all you had to do was work hard, keep quiet, educate yourself and your children, and when it was time, demand those rights. Even then there would be those who were irritated by Jews demanding anything, but there were more people who weren't. And if you didn't blow up anything or riot, you'd win in the end.

My mother went to a normal school, my father to Yale Law School. My mother never taught, my father never quite graduated. They were married too soon, their children came too fast. Existence became a struggle, one they could never really overcome. One way or another, it's all in this book. For example, in my real childhood, the hunger was painful. In *Li'l Abner* it was hilarious. The Dogpatch soil could produce only one crop—turnips—and every year the Turnip Termites, billions of them, would swoop down on Dogpatch and eat all the turnip blossoms. But the Yokums did have the Dogpatch ham,

and no matter how much of it you chewed off, you could sleep peacefully, for by morning it would have restored its juicy self.

My father was one of the most amusing of men, and he would draw, on brown paper bags, his triumphs over my mother. It was the only arena in which he won. He tried so hard, yet he was never able to quite support his family. My mother was a beautiful woman. I remember that from my early childhood. Yet photographs of her, in her thirties, show a saddened woman with white hair. In *Li'l Abner*, Abner's father, like mine, couldn't support his family, but he cheerfully gave that up, and let Mammy do it. In forty-three years we all knew that Mammy was the breadwinner, yet no one ever knew quite what she did. Or inquired. Abner, of course, was a mattress tester. He'd get up at 6 A.M., rush to the Little Wonder Mattress Company, flop down on one until noon, eat a hurried lunch, and then go back to sleep until six. It was a hard buck.

The Yokums lived in one place, where their grandparents had lived, and their great-grandparents before them. Was that because my family moved from one neighborhood to another, all around Connecticut, to Brooklyn, to Boston? My father's businesses constantly failed. He couldn't stand the shame of it, yet he knew that all he needed was a fresh start in a new city. And so we'd move, and after a year or two *that* business would fail. And so I grew up, in different cities, in different neighborhoods. I knew how bitter the struggle was for my parents, but I was fascinated by the changes.

I was also fascinated by the popular amusements of the time. We had no money to buy tickets to movies, but my brother Jerry, within hours of our arrival in any new neighborhood, knew exactly how to sneak into any new theater. With the movies of the thirties and forties, you knew where you were. The man with the open, honest face or the girl who was ready to die for her virginity were the heroes, and all the others were the villains. There was no nonsense about their villainy, no psychiatric alibis. They were rotten because they liked being rotten. Today, the good guys are motivated by the basest passions, the bad guys by the noblest; the little farm girl may have the heart of a whore, the streetwalker the ideals of an angel. How often the bad ones are played by our greatest stars, and the good ones by schlemiels!

Through the strip's forty-three years, we all knew the Yokums were the good guys. And yet, many of the bad guys became as popular as the Yokums. Not because they did anything good, but because they poured such imagination into their badness—and because we all knew they'd get theirs in the end. Take one story in this book, "The Eternal Bullmoose." General Bullmoose is at his physical peak, at ninety-nine the richest man on earth, but he worries about the day he'll have to leave his fabulous fortune to his son, Weakfish (the characters in *Li'l Abner* always had names that made any further description unnecessary). He orders that a giant head of himself be built, and pours into it all his knowledge of dirty tricks, loathsome schemes, and unspeakable double-dealings, and sends it to Weakfish. On the way it is hijacked by criminals. Now Bullmoose is confronted with the foulest of all enemies: himself! Can he come up with one more soul-sickening idea? Yes he can. Bullmoose was never more popular.

Li'l Abner was also shaped by my reading. At high school we were given *Ivanhoe* to read. It was like wading through cement. The other kids were sure it was a classic. I was sure it was muck. *Ivanhoe* made nonreaders of a generation of kids, but, happily, I had already read Dickens and Smollett and Twain, and I was protected. In the pages of the old *Saturday Evening Post*, I grew to know another fine author, Booth Tarkington. His main work was done many years before, but he was still charming enough for me to get that earlier work from our library. I read them all, with delight, from *Penrod* to *Theatre*.

At nine, I was run over by a trolley car. It severed my left leg at the hip. I came out of the hospital determined that this must make no difference. I strapped on a wooden leg and took my place in the neighborhood. There were some small changes. I could bat at baseball, but some other kid would run bases for me. I couldn't hop on trains, but I could still take off, by truck. I hadn't any clothes (teenagers then tried not to dress like bums), I had no car (and not the faintest chance to get the use of one, for I couldn't get a driving license), and I couldn't dance. Yet I wasted no time wishing I could. I looked for other diversions, friends who would share them with me. Now as I look back, I wonder if it wasn't because of the wooden leg, slowing me down, that I had the patience to study art. Before I was deep into my twenties I had become famous. I talked to interviewers fully about my wooden leg. But many forgot to mention it in their stories. Yet, how much of the sadness and the rage I suppressed in my teens stayed in me?

The artistic influences were any I saw, particularly the cartoons: *Barney Google, Jiggs and Maggie,* Goldberg cartoons. And then something hit the comic page, two new strips: *Dick Tracy* and *Little Orphan Annie.* No laughs. Plenty of terror. Breathless suspense. The nation's editors began demanding more. And that's when I came to New York from Boston.

I was twenty-three, I carried a mass of drawings, and I had nearly five dollars in my pocket. People were sleeping in alleys then, willing to work at anything, but I hadn't the faintest doubt I'd get a job. A widow on Twelfth Street in the Village said she'd trust me for the first week's rent. In gratitude, I did a charcoal drawing of her husband. He was a cop, killed in the line of duty. She gave me his photograph. He was a lummox, but that was my business. When the widow saw my picture, she was stunned. No one saw in him what only she and I saw. From that time on, not only was my rent never mentioned, but there were always little things waiting on my bedside table—apples, mints.

Nothing else in New York was coming through as well. I was crossing Eighth Avenue in the Fifties one day, my mind on my problems. A sportscar swerved and almost hit me. I was picking up my strips when the driver, a fat little man, asked, "You a cartoonist?" I gave him a surly yes.

He said, "I am, too. My name is Ham Fisher. I do *Joe Palooka.*" I grabbed his hand and shook it. I never cared much for his strip, but he was the first live cartoonist I had ever met. He asked, "You working?" I said I wasn't, and he said, "Come up to my studio." It was a small room in his penthouse. On the desk were several *Joe Palooka* Sunday pages. The fighters were decently drawn, but the girls seemed to be drawn by someone who had never seen a girl. "Do you think you could finish them?" I said I thought so. That was about four in the afternoon. At three the next morning he came in. I was still at it. He said, "Those girls aren't bad, and you inked in the fighters nicely." He gave me a ten-dollar bill and told me to "Come back tomorrow." And that's how it started.

I learned a great deal from Fisher. He had begun to go the way I knew cartoonists would have to go. He too loved the funny people, yet also realized that strips must now have suspense. Something to keep readers coming back. "Joe" was tall and blond, the heavyweight champion of the world. He fought three, four fights a year, and every fight built suspense. He was a simple character, surrounded by Broadway vultures, but protected, thank heaven, by the lowest of them all, his pal and manager, "Knobby Walsh." I worked for Fisher for twenty-five dollars a week, and I was grateful for it. I showed him in the next month or so that not only could I do the girls, but the fighters too. I could write stories and create new characters. He raised me to fifty, and he hinted that one day he might go to seventy-five. With that, I wrote my new wife, Catherine, to bring our new baby and come to New York. I'd find a place. As soon as they were there, Fisher began to change toward me. He demanded longer hours. He was terribly surly about my taking Saturday afternoons off. Now he had me. I changed too. Once I could think of no finer life than making seventy-five dollars a week doing Fisher's strip. He was making four thousand dollars a week. But now I knew I must get out. I didn't mind the long hours; I did mind being treated as a servant.

So nights at home, I began working on *Li'l Abner.* Oddly, I knew all my characters from Strip One. In forty-three years, there was never any basic change in them. Like Fisher's Joe, my Abner was a young man. And there the resemblance ended. Joe's background was Broadway glitter. Abner's background was Dogpatch hawgpens. I dove into lunacy. Fisher dipped his toe in it, carefully. We both did exactly what suited our temperaments. *Joe Palooka* had already attracted an enormous audience. *Li'l Abner* would, too. This was before the days of television. We cartoonists created all the great families. There was plenty of love and fame in the world, enough for both Fisher and me.

I brought the *Li'l Abner* samples up to King Features Syndicate and they offered me two hundred and fifty bucks a week, which was the equivalent of a thousand or more today. But the big guy there, Joe Connolly, said, "Great strip, great art, yes sir. A couple of things though: That Abner's an idiot! Make him a nice kid, with some saddle-shoes on him. And Daisy Mae's pretty, but how about some pretty clothes? As a matter of fact, why not forget the mountain bit and move them all to New Jersey? And that Mammy, she's got to go. You need a sweet, white-haired lady."

Well, I thought about all that and I realized he wanted *Polly and Her Pals!* But I also had two hundred and fifty dollars a week. I was pretty sick about it. I walked up to United Feature—Monte Bourjaily was the head of it then—and they looked at it and showed it to their salesmen. They were young and daring. They wanted to take it out just as it was. They offered me fifty bucks a week, which was the lowest they paid, and I grabbed it and forgot King Features, because I was now able to do my own strip exactly as I wanted to do it.

This book begins with Abner's marriage to Daisy Mae. That sequence gives you Abner as he was and as he became. His main interest from the beginning was in not getting married. His Mammy's main interest was in getting him married, and to Daisy Mae Scragg. In New York (in forty-three years, Abner has been to New York, as well as to London and Paris, more times than Secretary Vance, yet he is always a gawking stranger), he meets Bet-a-Million Bashby, who has achieved a colossal fortune by one simple rule: "Always bet on a sure thing, and

always bet with a fool." Bashby bets that an elderly man can safely cross a street where all traffic is forbidden. Abner bets that he can't. The man starts. A hydrant blows up. Abner wins. All through the years Bashby bet on sure things, and all through the years Abner won.

In 1944 the first Sinatra craze was on. Sinatra was a friend. I created Hal Fascinatra, Abner as a starved-

down front for Concertino Constipato, a singer with a million dollars worth of talent and a dime's worth of appeal. Sinatra loved it. A few years later, I did one about Liberace, also a friend. I called the character Loverboynik (see "Ketch a Critic by th' Toe"). Liberace was cut to the quick. But most of Abner's complicated problems were worked out with a regular cast: his parents (Pappy could do nothing, which was what his family expected of him, and Mammy could do anything, and that was all she was expected to do), Lonesome Polecat and Hairless Joe (they manufactured Kickapoo Joy

Juice—if it needs more body, throw a body in), Joe Btfsplk (the world's most loving friend and worst jinx), Available Jones (anything for a price), Earthquake Mc-Goon (the world's dirtiest wrestler), Fearless Fosdick (the ideal of every one hundred percent red-blooded American boy), Moonbeam McSwine and her Pappy (who raised her in as fine a way as he raised his hogs), Smilin' Zack (who preferred people to be quiet—really quiet, not breathing or anything), Barney Barnsmell (loneliest boy in town on account of his job, which was Inside Man at the Skunkworks), Evil-Eye Fleegle (whose quadruple whammy could melt a battleship), Orson Waggon (at seven he had written more melancholy novels than Tolstoy, louder operas than Wagner), and on.

In April, 1946, Abner discovered Lower Slobbovia, where the favorite dish is polar bears and vice-versa. In August, 1948, out of the Valley of the Shmoon came the Shmoo, billions of them, who gave mankind everything it needed and so had to be destroyed because they were bad for business.

After avoiding Daisy Mae for eighteen years, Li'l Abner married her, convinced to the end that it was all a silly dream. A year later, in 1953, after a pregnancy that ambled on so long that readers began sending me medical books, a baby was born, "Honest Abe" Yokum. And in 1954, "Tiny" Yokum arrived. (Fifteen and a half years

before, Mammy had collapsed in a neighbor's house feeling rotten. She woke up in much better shape, and left. Happening to be in Dogpatch for the first time since then, the neighbor returned the baby Mammy had had in her house.)

I had grown up in days when anybody who ate regularly (the upper class) felt no responsibility for the poor souls who didn't, and helped them only out of human kindness. As I grew into the upper class, I became a liberal. We demanded that the unfortunate be given welfare, that their rent be paid, that they be given food benefits. We fought for all that, and slowly, painfully, we won. It was marvelous being a liberal in those days, because you were on the side of humanity.

What began to bother me, privately, was that, as things grew better, the empire of the needy seemed to grow larger. Somehow, they became entitled to government gifts other people couldn't get, such as people who worked. Yet, I remained a loyal liberal. I lived in Cambridge, Massachusetts, the home of liberalism. I spoke at liberal banquets in New York, Los Angeles, Washington. One day a lady photographer came to my studio and showed me a collection of Boston photographs. A publisher would publish them if only I would rattle off the captions. She had brought a tape recorder. Well, one doesn't turn down a lady liberal. The pictures were funny. My captions tried to be. And then we came to the last one. This one, she said, will break your heart. She showed me a picture of a city street. It was mid-afternoon, the sun was shining. Garbage cans were tipped on the sidewalk. Bottles lined the gutters. On a porch sprawled a half dozen teenagers, drinking and smoking. The caption, I said, should be, "Get up off your asses and clean up your street!" The lady stormed out. I guess that was when I began leaving what liberalism had become.

My politics didn't change. I had always been for those who were despised, disgraced, and denounced by other people. That was what had changed. Suddenly it was the poor working bastard who was being denounced. He had always worked, his wife had always worked, his kids worked. At some point they bought a house in the suburbs. It was from his paycheck that the billions for welfare came. He never complained about it. But why were the others complaining about him? He was never a silent generation; he was a bewildered one. I knew that it would be terribly unsmart to say anything in his defense. But I knew that if I remained silent, I would die as a satirist. A satirist has only one gift: he sees where the fraud and fakery are. I turned around and let the other side have it.

It's been an exhilarating forty-three years.

Al Capp

The Wedding

     The Wedding

The Wedding

The Wedding

The Wedding

"Ketch a Critic by th' Toe"

24

"Ketch a Critic by th' Toe"

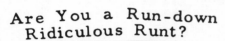

"Ketch a Critic by th' Toe"

"Ketch a Critic by th' Toe"

L-LOOK!!- THAT **KID** LIFTED THAT HUGE MASS OF BLUBBER!!

GET HIM OFF!!- **I'LL** PICK "MR. BEAUTIFUL, OF 1956"!!

AS SPOKESMAN FOR THE CROWD, YOU'D BETTER NOT PICK ANYONE BUT **THAT KID!!**

WHO?- ME?-

RIGHT!!- YOU'RE MORE MAN THAN ANYONE ON THAT STAGE.!!

SHECKS!!-AH IS NO MAN. AH IS MERELY 15½ Y'ARS OLD!!

I CROWN YOU, TINY YOKUM, "MR. BEAUTIFUL, OF 1956"!!

THANK YO', LADIES AN' GENNULMEN-

TH' WAY AH GOT MAH WONDIFUL BUILT IS MAINLY BY **RESTIN'.** ME AN' A FEW PIGS SPENDS MOST O' OUR TIME LYIN' UNDER APPLE TREES.

TH' PIGS IS SOOTHIN' COMPANY, AN' TH' APPLES IS MIGHTY HEALTHFUL, IF THEY HAPPENS T'FALL IN YORE MOUF-

10-8

YES, FOLKS.!!- YO', TOO, KIN GIT A WONDIFUL BUILT, LIKE AH GOT.!! SLEEP A LOT, EAT A LOT, ASSOSHEEATE WIF TH' RIGHT TYPE O' PIGS- AN' NEVAH DO **NO** WORK!!-

10-9

THET'LL WEAR YORE MUSCLES OUT-URGLE!!-

SORRY, MR. BEAUTIFUL, BUT LOVERBOYNIK, "SWEETHEART OF THE PIANO", IS ON NEXT!!

IN FACT, HERE HE IS.!!

YOU'RE **JUST** THE MAN I WANT TO SEE!!

SHECKS!!- AH HAIN'T NO MAN, "SWEETHEART O' TH' PIANO". AH IS MERELY A BOY, 15½ Y'ARS OLE!!

ALTHOUGH I AM THE IDEAL OF EVERY UPSET AMERICAN GIRL-

OH, YO' SHORE IS, SWEETHEART OF TH' PIANO.

I, FRANKLY, DON'T SEEM TO ATTRACT MANY **MEN** TO MY CONCERTS. MAYBE YOU, MR. BEAUTIFUL, ARE THE ANSWER-

I HAVE A GORGEOUS IDEA FOR A **NEW** ACT.!!- IT GOES LIKE THIS- PSST!!-PSST!!-

GASP!!-YO' IS A **GENIUS,** TO OF THUNK **THAT** UP.!!-LE'S GO!!

1040

28   **"Ketch a Critic by th' Toe"**

"Ketch a Critic by th' Toe"

"Ketch a Critic by th' Toe"

"Ketch a Critic by th' Toe"

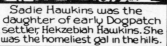

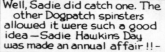

"Ketch a Critic by th' Toe"

"Ketch a Critic by th' Toe"

The Descent and Rise
of Edward R. Mushroom

The Descent and Rise of Edward R. Mushroom

The Descent and Rise of Edward R. Mushroom

The Descent and Rise of Edward R. Mushroom

The Descent and Rise of Edward R. Mushroom

The Descent and Rise of Edward R. Mushroom

The Descent and Rise of Edward R. Mushroom

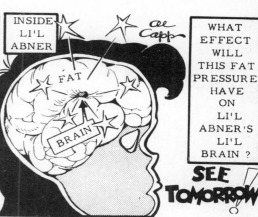

The Descent and Rise of Edward R. Mushroom

Small wonder Edward R. Mushroom gets that squashed feeling!! A veritable mountain of fat is smothering his Memory Muscle.

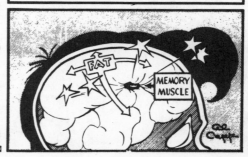

The Descent and Rise of Edward R. Mushroom

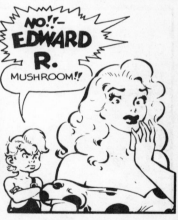

The Descent and Rise of Edward R. Mushroom

The Descent and Rise of Edward R. Mushroom

The Descent and Rise of Edward R. Mushroom

FLOWER OF AMERICAN FIGHTHOOD PANICS AT SIGHT OF BOOMCHIK

N.Y. City: Fleeing in terror from the shaking fist and mocking laugh of the Russian Champion, Boomchik, are America's most fearless fighters!! *15*

ANOTHER INSULTING NOTE FROM RUSSIA

Washington, D.C.—The State Department today received the following cable from Moscow. "The Champion of Russia, Boomchik, will arrive tomorrow, at Idlewild Airport, to challenge the decadent capitalistic champions of the —PTUI!—U.S.A.", to a fight to decide once and for all which is the better way of life."

N.Y. Stock Exchange

PRESIDENT CALLS ON ALL AMERICAN PRIZEFIGHTERS TO DEFEND OUR PRESTIGE

N.Y. City: Champions of all weights, waiting at airport to accept insulting challenge of Russian Champion, Boomchik, whose plane is expected to arrive at any

PANIC AT IDLEWILD AIRPORT!!

N.Y. City: The fist in the upper left corner is Boomchik, the Russian Champion. Reading from left to right are all of America's toughest prizefighters!!

FLOWER OF AMERICAN FIGHTHOOD PANICS AT SIGHT OF BOOMCHIK

N.Y. City: Fleeing in terror from the shaking fist and mocking laugh of the Russian Champion, Boomchik, are America's most fearless fighters!!

12-15

LISSEN!!—IT'S "TH' VOICE OF MOSCOW," COMIN' IN ON SHORT WAVE.!!—

WE LAFF ON YOU FACES, DECADENT CAPITALIST SWINE.!!—YOU RUNNING FROM BOOMCHIK LIKE YELLOW DUCKS!!—NOW, WHICH IS TOP COUNTRY? HA HA HA.!! HO HO HO!!—

OH!! EF ONLY **AH** WERE A MAN!!

ALTHOUGH ALL AMERICA'S GREATEST PRIZEFIGHTERS HAVE FLED IN TERROR FROM THE RUSSIAN CHAMPION, BOOMCHIK——

12-16

—AMERICAN PRESTIGE MAY **YET** BE SAVED.!!—HERE COMES A STRONG, MANLY FIGURE.!! IT—**GASP!!**—LOOKS LIKE JOHN WAYNE !!

AMERICA **IS** SAVED!!

HE STRIDES INTO BOOMCHIK'S ROOM.!! **WHAT** WILL HAPPEN?

WHUT **KIN** HAPPEN WIF JOHN WAYNE ON TH' JOB?

WHUT **ALLUS** HAPPENS, WHEN **HE** SWINGS INTO ACK-SHUN?

SOMEONE, WHO LOOKED **MIGHTY** LIKE JOHN WAYNE, JUST STRODE INTO BOOMCHIK'S ROOM.!!

AMERICAN PRESTIGE IS **SAVED**!!

SNAP!!

AH SEEN JOHN WAYNE CLEAN UP VILLAINS SINCE AH WERE A **KID**.!!

12-17

HE'LL MOP UP TH' FLOOR WIF THET—

SHOOSH, PAPPY!! HE'S COMIN' OUT.!!

S/R.!! DID YOU···

I—I D-DIDN'T LAY A **FINGER** ON BOOMCHIK.!!—I D-DIDN'T D-**DARE**.!!—

A BLACK-HAIRED BOY, WHO LOOKED AN—**UGH!**—AWFUL LOT LIKE **FABIAN**, JUST BRAVELY ENTERED BOOMCHIK'S ROOM——

—AND HERE HE SLINKS OUT!!—HIS HAIR IS **SNOW WHITE!!**

12-19

8 HOURS LATER—

SO MANY—**SOB.!!**—FINE AMERICANS HAVE FACED BOOMCHIK, AND **LEFT**—WITHOUT **ACCEPTING THE CHALLENGE!!**—GENE TUNNEY, BARNEY BARUCH, BARNEY ROSS, BRODERICK CRAWFORD, ALF LANDON AND ROY COHN.!!

ROY COHN, **TOO**?—TSK! TSK!!

First Living Color Section

The Bashful Bulganik

A Letter from Wyatt Yokum

Cap'n Eddie Flies Again

The Eternal Bullmoose

Welcome Strangers

Mary Worm

Steve Cantor

Crumbumbo's Ultimate Weapon

The Bashful Bulganik

A Letter from Wyatt Yokum

Cap'n Eddie Flies Again

The Eternal Bullmoose

The Eternal Bullmoose

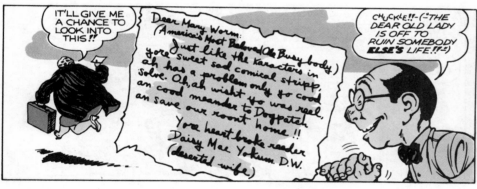

Mary Worm/Steve Cantor

Mary Worm/Steve Cantor

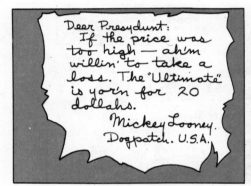

Crumbumbo's Ultimate Weapon

Crumbumbo's Ultimate Weapon

A Common
Femmy-nine Ailment

Mockaroni

MEANWHILE: BACK AT THE MOCKARONI RANCH—

ROCK HUSTLER KEEPS AXIN' FO' MORE AN' **MORE** MOCKARONI.*!*

MUS' BE A FEARFUL PLAGUE O' FATOCEROSES IN TH' REST O' TH' U.S.A.*!*

WE OUGHTA BE SEEIN' THAR SKELETONS FLOATIN' BY, OVERHEAD, ANY DAY, NOW *!*

Tm. Reg. U. S. Pat Off.—All rights reserved
Copr. 1961 by United Feature Syndicate, Inc.

LOOK, MAMMY— **THAR'S** SOME *!!*

GASP!—**THEM** HAIN'T NO FATOCEROSES!! THEM'S HOOMIN BEANS—**SAME AS WE IS!!**

ROCK HUSTLER DONE TRICKED US!!

7-7

THEM'S **FOLKS,** SAME AS WE IS!!

ROCK HUSTLER DONE **BETRAYED** US!! HE BIN SELLIN' MOCKARONI TO **PEOPLE!!**

WHY—THASS UNLEGAL, UNDECENT, UNHOOMIN, AN' PROB'LY **UNAMERICAN!!**

7-8   Tm. Reg. U. S. Pat Off.—All rights reserved
Copr. 1961 by United Feature Syndicate, Inc.

BLAST YOU!! I HAVEN'T RECEIVED A SHIPMENT OF MOCKARONI FOR **2 DAYS,** NOW!!—

??-WHAT'S THAT SMOKE?

TH' MOCKARONI FIELDS!!—**WE BURNED 'EM DOWN!!**

7-10   Tm. Reg. U. S. Pat Off.—All rights reserved
Copr. 1961 by United Feature Syndicate, Inc.

Y-YOU MEAN, IT'S **ALL** GONE? **ULP!!**

NOT QUITE!! WE SAVED 'NUFF FO' **YO'!!** EAT!! EAT!!

-CHUCKLE!- NOW HE'LL CRAVE MORE!!

IT'S **DELICIOUS!!** MORE!! MORE!!

MORE MOCKARONI!! -SMACK!- DROOL!!- -SLOBBER!- MORE **!!**

EAT AWAY!! THAR'S 'NUFF LEFT FO' YO'— FO' A **WEEK**—

—AN' THASS -CHUCKLE!!—ALL YO'LL NEED !!— GOO'BYE, ROCK HUSTLER!!— WE'LL BE SEEIN' YO'!!

7-11

ONE WEEK LATER.

THAR HE GOES!! RIGHT ON SCHEDULE!!

HE MIGHT BE TH' **FUST** MAN TO LAND ON TH' MOON!!

Indian Love Call

The Lips of Marcia Perkins

The Lips of Marcia Perkins

The Lips of Marcia Perkins

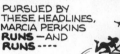

The Lips of Marcia Perkins

The Lips of Marcia Perkins

The Lips of Marcia Perkins

The Lips of Marcia Perkins

Snapples

Snapples

Snapples

Second Living Color Section

Fleegle's Last Whammy

We Who Are About to Dial

The Gorging of Stupefyin' Jones

Bone with the Wind

Fearless Fosdick Meets Dr. Doolittlegood

The Fowler Cometh

FLEEGLE DOES NOT REALIZE THAT THE LITTLE JOIK IS **JUST** AS POWERFUL AS HE IS, IN HIS OWN HUMBLE WAY.
HE IS JOE BTFSPLK, THE WORLD'S WORST JINX. **D**ISASTER COMES TO WHOEVER JOE IS NEAR.

Fleegle's Last Whammy

Fleegle's Last Whammy

Fleegle's Last Whammy

Fleegle's Last Whammy

We Who Are About to Dial

The Gorging of Stupefyin' Jones

9-13

The Gorging of Stupefyin' Jones

Fearless Fosdick Meets Dr. Doolittlegood

THE OFFICE OF THE EDITOR OF DOGPATCH COUNTY'S LEADING PAPER — "THE WEST PORK CHOP OBSERVER"

OUR RIVAL, "THE NEWS", HAS **DOUBLED** ITS CIRCULATION SINCE THEY STARTED THIS COLUMN!!

Evening Edition

Nan Glanders

Advice for the Heart-sick!!

Dear Nan:

WE'VE GOT TO START ONE!! — BUT, WHO'LL **WRITE** IT?

DON'T LOOK AT **ME**!! — I'VE GOT A **WEAK STOMACH**!!

A GENTLEMAN TO SEE YOU, SIR — WITH A LETTER OF INTRODUCTION!!

State Penitentiary

Office of the Warden

Dear Jim:

Knowing your interest in rehabilitation, I am sending you a paroled bigamist, B. Fowler McNest. He was married to 22 women, in 22 states---simultaneously.

Maybe there is something on the paper, that you could find, for

B. FOWLER McNEST OUGHT TO KNOW MORE ABOUT MARRIAGE THAN **ANYONE**!! — CALL HIM IN!!

OH, **NO** — UGH!! — **NO**!! — **NOBODY'D** TAKE ADVICE FROM ANYONE WHO LOOKS LIKE **THAT**!!

WHY LET ANYONE **KNOW** WHAT HE LOOKS LIKE? — OR EVEN THAT HE'S A **"HE"**. LET'S RUN HIS COLUMN UNDER A **GIRL'S** NAME!!

LIKE — HMMM!— "HAZEL HOMEWRECKER"?!

—AND RUN A SWEET PICTURE WITH IT— HOW ABOUT THIS ONE? — SHE WAS ELECTED "MISS SYMPATHY." OF 1955.

Tm. Reg. U S Pat Off — All rights reserved
Copr. 1963 by United Feature Syndicate, Inc.

ONE MONTH LATER.

??—WHUT'S MAKIN' YO' CRY?

HAZEL HOMEWRECKER'S COLUMN. **WHUT** A LIFE SHE MUST LEAD!!

SHE GITS **SO** MANY ONHAPPY LETTERS FUM MIZZUBLE WIVES — SHE MUST THINK **THAR HAIN'T A HAPPY MARRIAGE IN ALL TH' WORLD**!!

THEN, YO' WRITE HER HOW HAPPY **OUR** MARRIAGE IS!! — AND SEND HER A PITCHER OF CONTENTED US!!

AND, WITH THIS SUGGESTION, ABNER DOOMS HIMSELF TO A HIDEOUS FATE — AND BREAKS UP HIS HOME!!

5-5

The Fowler Cometh

153

HAZEL HOMEWRECKER, TH' LOVE ADVICE COLUMNIST, GITS **SO** MANY LETTERS, 'BOUT ONHAPPY MARRIAGES, AH WRIT HER 'BOUT A **HAPPY** ONE---

—NAMELY **OUR'N**!! EVEN SENT HER OUR PITCHER!! HOPE IT BRIGHTENS UP HER DAY!!

IT DOESN'T MERELY BRIGHTEN UP HAZEL —IT **INFLAMES HER!!** FOR THIS IS THE PEN-NAME OF THE PAROLED BIGAMIST **B. FOWLER McNEST!!**

(—SHE BRINGS BACK MY OLD CRAVING—! TO **MARRY**!!"—)

SCIENCE EDITOR

'ER—I'M INTERESTED IN THAT ARTICLE YOU WROTE, LAST WEEK— ABOUT **DEEP-FREEZONE**!!

IT'S A POWDER USED IN THE TROPICS---

—WHERE THEY HAVE NO DEEP-FREEZES. IT DOES THE **SAME THING**!! IT'S TASTELESS—

IT'S PUT IN THE FOOD OF CHICKENS AND COWS—AND IN **ONE WEEK**---

THE LIVESTOCK **KEELS OVER**, APPARENTLY **DEAD!!** ACTUALLY THEY'RE SIMPLY FROZEN STIFF!! THE EFFECT LASTS **30 DAYS**—

TASTELESS, EH? AND THE VICTIM IS—APPARENTLY DEAD, FOR---**30 DAYS**?—THANKS—

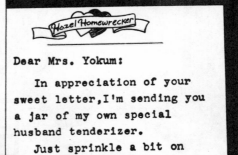

Hazel Homewrecker

Dear Mrs. Yokum:

　In appreciation of your sweet letter, I'm sending you a jar of my own special husband tenderizer.

　Just sprinkle a bit on your husband's food

and I promise you he'll think it's real cool.

Sincerely,

Hazel

IT WAS MIGHTY ROUGH, FRYIN' THEM PO'K CHOPS, IN THIS HEAT WAVE!!

HEAT WAVE? AH IS F-FREEZIN'!!

— **TWO DAYS LATER** —

TH' PAPER SAYS TH' HEAT WAVE'S GONNA **CORN-TINUE!!**

HEAT WAVES HAIN'T-**SHIVER!!**-**CHATTER!**-**SHAKE!!**-WHUT THEY **USED** TO BE.!!

5-19

TO BE CONTINUED:

The Fowler Cometh

156

The Fowler Cometh

The Fowler Cometh

6-23

TO BE CONTINUED:

160   **The Fowler Cometh**

Ignoble Savages

Porknoy's Complaint

Who's Who in Pork ®

Fatback

J. Roaringham Fatback: "King of Pork". Born in Hammond, Indiana. Educated at **Sow Western** University. Merged his tiny **FCC** *(Fatback's Chops and Cutlets)* with **IBCo.** *(International Bacon)* and became most prominent figure in the world of Swine. Resides on Pork Ave., New York — and summers at **Newpork, Rhode Island.** His fire and sparkle have always

YOU'VE CORNERED THE WORLD'S SUPPLY OF **BEANS!!**

NOW I'M THE KING OF PORK **AND** BEANS!!

YOU'VE CORNERED THE WORLD'S **BEAN** SUPPLY —

—WHICH MAKES ME THE KING OF PORK **AND** BEANS!!

IT DOESN'T MEAN MUCH IN A **MATERIAL** WAY — A BILLION OR TWO — BUT IT HAS **SENTIMENTAL** SIGNIFICANCE —

I DIDN'T **ALWAYS** OWN ISLANDS — YACHTS!! — I WAS ONCE A MISERABLE LITTLE SWINE!!

--once?--

AS A POVERTY-STRICKEN LI'L NIPPER, **I** HAD PORK AND BEANS **ONLY** ON CHRISTMAS! **OTHER** KIDS HAD IT **EVERY** DAY --

—BUT NOW I'M THE PORK AND BEAN KING!! NOT THAT I WANT TO BE A SWINE ABOUT THIS--

—BUT **NOW** THEY'LL HAVE TO PAY **MY** PRICES, FOR THEIR **DAILY PORK AND BEANS!!**

(--"HE'S LIVING IN THE **LAST CENTURY!!** — DOESN'T HE KNOW IT'S BEEN REPLACED AS THE FAVORITE AMERICAN DISH—BY **PIZZA?**")

YOU TELL HIM!!

ME? WITH MY HEART CONDITION?

I **CAN'T!!** I'M **NON VIOLENT!!**

TOMORROW I RETIRE ON A PENSION!! I'LL DO IT—

OFFICE PRESID

MR. F-FATBACK, SIR --- P-PORK AND BEANS **ISN'T** THE MOST POPULAR AMERICAN DISH ANY MORE — **PIZZA** IS!!

YOU'RE FIRED!! — AND I DON'T PAY PENSIONS TO **TRAITORS!!**

WHAT AN IRONIC JOKE!!

WHILE **YOU** WERE CONNIVING AND CONSPIRING TO BECOME THE **PORK AND BEANS KING**--

-**PORK AND BEANS** WAS REPLACED AS OUR NATIONAL DISH--BY **PIZZA**!!

A **TRUE KING** DOESN'T ABDICATE TO **PIZZA-CRAZED PEASANTS**!!

I WILL RESTORE PORK AND BEANS TO ITS RIGHTFUL THRONE ON THE AMERICAN DINNER TABLE !!

10-2

ANNUAL "DISH OF THE YEAR" CONTEST STARTS IN PARIS !!

The world's leading food manufacturers, accompanied by the world's greatest chefs, are arriving in Paris to compete for the title.

The winner traditionally becomes the world's most popular dish–and

PORK AND BEANS MUST WIN !!

IT **CAN**, MR. FATBACK, IF YOU FOLLOW **THIS ANCIENT RECIPE** !!

IT HAS **ONE** DRAW-BACK, DAD–

IT BORDERS ON **CANNIBALISM**!!

SOME PEOPLE THINK IT'S **WORSE**!!

10-3

~Ye Ancient Masticator~
Porke and Beanes Buckingham Palace Style —

Take ye fleshe of ye Hammus Alabammus (an incredibly tender swyne, found only in Dogpatche) and blend with ye fleshe of ye Wilde Boare in its most wildly romanticke state, which occureth when it reacheth ye age of Boare Mitzvah.

This mingling of tendernesse and toughnesse resulteth in a dish so savory and seductive it surpasseth ye dreames of mortal man, when joined with Beanes !! —

10-4

© 1969 by News Syndicate Co. Inc.
World Rights Reserved

PIZZA? MORE POPULAR THAN **PORK AND BEANS?**

OUR RESEARCH **PROVES** IT SIR–

PIZZA
PORK AND BEANS

IT PROVES **YOU'RE A BUNCH OF COMMUNISTS**!!

I'LL HAVE THE RESEARCH DONE BY SOME **100 PERCENT AMERICANS**!!

HE DOES–AND--

WHERE IS HE GOING .IN HIS WORLD WAR II HELMET?

TO **FATBACK'S**– **HIS** RESEARCH CAME OUT PIZZA TOO !!

9-29

174

Porknoy's Complaint

EASY TO -SNIFF!- TELL WHO SHE'S SCOOTIN' OUT TO PLAY WIF!! THAT FAV'RITE O' ALL LOCAL LI'L SWINE—MOONBEAM!!

10-13

© 1969 by News Syndicate Co. Inc. World Rights Reserved

GASP!!

PORKNOY!!— OH!! IT COULD BE FATAL TO MAKE THAT MISTAKE AGIN, SALOMEY!!

Al Capp

DAISY MAE SWORE OUT A COMPLAINT AGIN PORKNOY!!

HE TRIED TO LURE SWEET, INNERCENT LI'L SALOMEY—

10-14

—TO "KISSIN' ROCK"!!

1969 by News Syndicate Co. Inc. World Rights Reserved

LIKE SOME GARBAGE, PORKNOY?

IT'S THE FINEST!! —MY PERSONAL LEAVINGS—

—BUT PORKNOY DOESN'T TRUST PEOPLE—

Al Capp

NOTHING TO BE AFRAID OF!! JUST A FRIENDLY PLATE OF SWILL—

H-HERE COMES AN ARMED POSSE!!

SEEN ANY FILTHY BEASTS 'ROUND HERE?

NOT UNTIL YOU FOLKS CAME ALONG—

THANKS— WE'LL TROMP ON!!

10-15

1969 by News Syndicate Co. Inc. World Rights Reserved

Al Capp

"I CAN TRUST THOSE CITY GUYS" GRUNTS PORKNOY TO HIMSELF—

IF YO' IS APPROACHED BY A SWINE—

—WIF A ROTTEN COM-PLECK-SHUN, A TREMENJUS SNOUT, AN' TH' MANNERS OF A PIG—

© 1969 by News Syndicate Co. Inc. World Rights Reserved

10-16

—RUN, SALOMEY— IT'LL BE PORKNOY!!

—MEANWHILE—

WE'RE YOUR BUDDIES PORKNOY—

WE'LL CLEAR UP YOUR COMPLEXION, GIVE YOU A SNOUT JOB, AND TEACH YOU LOVELY MANNERS—

Al Capp

Porknoy's Complaint

"FATBACK DONE RESTORED MAH FAITH IN HUMANS" GRUNTS PORKNOY TO HIMSELF!!

"THANKS TO HIM SALOMEY'S NOW -SNORT!- -DROOL!- TRUSTIN'LY HEADED FO' -PANT- PANT!!- KISSIN' ROCK WIF ME--

10-22

SUDDENLY EVERYTHING GOES BLACK!!

ALL CRATED AND READY TO BE SHIPPED TO FATBACK.!!

THE INGREDIENTS FOR YOUR "PORK AND BEANS- BUCKINGHAM PALACE STYLE" HAVE ARRIVED MR. FATBACK!!

MY IMPOSSIBLE DREAM WILL COME TRUE!!

I CAN ALMOST TASTE THEIR TENDER MORSELS—FLOATING IN A SIMMERING POT OF GOLDEN BEANS!!

10-23

WHAT'S WRONG WITH MR. FATBACK?

HE'S BOUGHT A THRONE, A CROWN, AND A SCEPTRE—

10-24

HE THINKS HE'S A KING!!

I WILL BE A KING!! KING OF PORK AND BEANS!! AND YOU, SALOMEY AND PORKNOY WILL MAKE ME ONE!!

ALL RIGHT, FATBACK!!-I'M ON MY KNEES - BUT I STILL SAY YOU'RE NO KING!!

HO! HO!!-BUT I WILL BE!! KING OF PORK AND BEANS!!-I'LL WIN THAT PRIZE IN PARIS, BY COMBINING THE TENDER FLESH OF THAT HAMMUS ALABAMMUS....

10-25

-WITH THE RUGGED RUMP OF THAT WILDLY ROMANTIC WILD BOAR---

-AND FATBACK'S PORK AND BEANS WILL BECOME "DISH OF THE YEAR!! EVERYONE WILL PAY TRIBUTE TO ME!!

Porknoy's Complaint

177

Porknoy's Complaint

A MAN'S LIFE IS WASTED, UNLESS HIS LIFE'S DREAM COMES TRUE.!! - **TRUE?**

TRUE!!

11-18

THEN A **REAL** MAN SHOULD GIVE HIS **LIFE** TO HIS DREAM.!!

THASS DEE.P, FATBACK—

VERY-SOB!- DEEP!!

HERE'S TOMMY!!

(-"HE LOOKS CHEERFUL TONIGHT. HE WON'T HAVE TO HOLD UP HIS OWN PRODUCTS.!!-")

© 1970 by News Syndicate Co. Inc World Rights Reserved 2-11

The Tommy Wholesome Show

Backstage at the Tommy Wholesome show—

HOW DO YOU LIKE THESE NEW SIGNS?

DEAFENING APPLAUSE

CONVULSIVE LAUGHTER FOLLOWED BY STANDING OVATION!!

INSANE GIGGLING, BUILDING INTO UNCONTROLLABLE HYSTERIA

WILD CHEERS INTERSPERSED WITH SCREAMS OF DELIGHT!!

FINE.!!-BUT REMEMBER!! HOLD 'EM UP, **ONLY** WHEN TOMMY SPEAKS !!

WHEN ANYONE **ELSE** DOES, I HOLD **THIS** ONE UP- RIGHT?—

DEATHLY QUIET!!

2-2

© 1970 by News Syndicate Co. Inc. World Rights Reserved

???- BOB HIP ON MY SHOW?

—BUT **HIS** JOKES GOT MORE LAUGHS THAN **MINE**, LAST TIME HE WAS ON.!!

THEY WON'T TONIGHT, BOSS.!! EVERY TIME HE GETS TO A GAG LINE, **WE'LL** INTERRUPT WITH **721** IMPORTANT MESSAGES, FOLLOWED BY **905** SPOT ANNOUNCE-MENTS!!

HE'LL LOOK LIKE A CRASHING BORE— AND THESE AD LIBS WILL MAKE **YOU** LOOK LIKE THE NEW **BERNARD SHAW !!**

2-3

© 1970 by News Syndicate Co. Inc. World Rights Reserved

The Tommy Wholesome Show

The Tommy Wholesome Show

185

The Tommy Wholesome Show

The Tommy Wholesome Show

TOMMY WHOLESOME SHOW PRODUCTS TO BE ADVERTISED IN THE FIRST ¼-HOUR

HOP IN!!

3-4

COMFY?

PERFECTLY—EXCEPT I'M UPSIDE DOWN—

Fro-Uppy Puppy Food!!

© 1970 by News Syndicate Co. Inc.
World Rights Reserved

PSST-YO' IS TH' FUST COMMERSHUL!! WHEN HE OPENS TH' BOX, STAND UP AN' SING YORE POVERTY-STRICKEN LI'L HEART OUT!!—

AND NOW THAT THE LADY ANTHROPOLOGIST HAS EXPLAINED HOW HARMLESS HEROIN IS FOR CHILDREN···

© 1970 by News Syndicate Co. Inc.
World Rights Reserved

—LET'S HEAR FROM OUR NEXT GUEST—THE PRIME MINISTER OF—
—??-OOPS!!—

3-5

TIME FOR A REALLY IMPORTANT MESSAGE—FROM THE FRO-UPPY PUPPY FOOD COMPANY!!

(—"HERE COME SKEETS' BIG CHANCE!!—)

I KNOW YOU FLEW IN FROM EUROPE FOR YOUR 2½-SECOND IN-DEPTH INTERVIEW, PRIME MINISTER———

© 1970 by News Syndicate Co. Inc.
World Rights Reserved

—BUT THERE'S NO TIME—WITH THIS 42-MINUTE COMMERCIAL COMING UP—

3-6

STILL IT WON'T BE A TOTAL LOSS!! HE MIGHT PERSONALLY SAY "GOOD NIGHT" TO YOU!!

H-HE MIGHT?

Fro-Uppies

AND NOW, A TREAT FOR YOUR DOG!!

HI-HO!

Fro-Uppy PUPPY FOOD

3-7

MOR-RIS!!—RAMBLING NOSE OF THE WILDWOOD!!—YOUR FRAGRANCE DIVINE WITH MINE WILL ENTWINE!!

Fro-Uppy Puppy Food

IT'S SKEETS CHARLESTON!! ISN'T HE DEAD?

I THINK SO!! LISTEN———

© 1970 by News Syndicate Co. Inc.
World Rights Reserved

The Tommy Wholesome Show